ULTIMATE ACTIVITY BOOK

By Sheri Tan

INSIGHT
KIDS

San Rafael · Los Angeles · London

Excitement, adventure, and surprises wait for you in the Game of LIFE! Are you a risk-taker or more of a wait-and-see kind of person? One thing's for sure: It's going to be a unique journey!

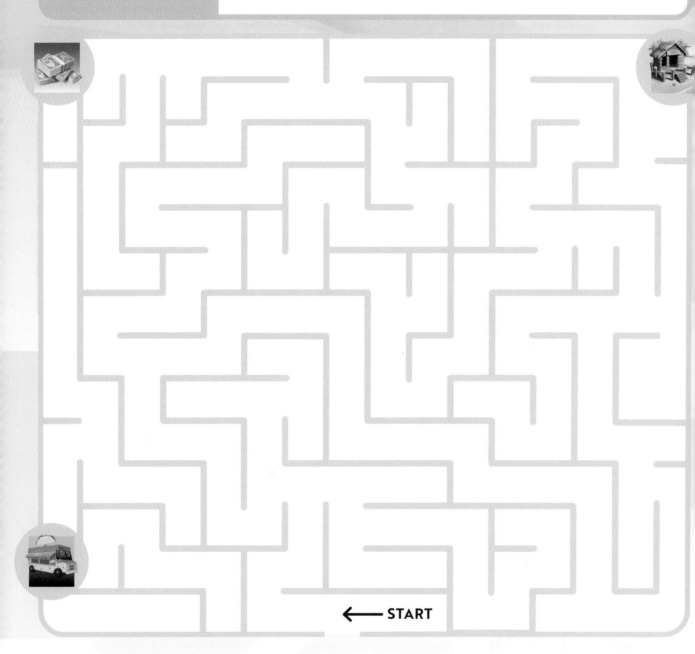

← START

FORGE YOUR PATH!

Will you live by the beach, have your own taco truck, or find a huge pile of money? Let's find out!

```
Z V X X M X M S S S H S
A R J E X M C S M O Y C
N R O N P I L O T L I D
A E C T A M N F X D E E
I B V H I I O D E I Y N
R R J M I N C M W E E T
A A H U N T A I W R T I
N B D U D R E J G R C S
I G R I A G C C Q A K T
R S W P I K E K T I M A
E R E T H G I F E R I F
T N A I C I R T C E L E
E A C C O U N T A N T C
V J H F B R E H C A E T
```

NURSE	PARAMEDIC	ELECTRICIAN	DENTIST
FIREFIGHTER	PILOT	JANITOR	TEACHER
MAGICIAN	ARCHITECT	ACCOUNTANT	BARBER
VETERINARIAN	SOLDIER	JUDGE	

JOB HUNTING

Look for the 15 jobs that are listed in the word bank. You can find the words in all directions in the word search: across, down, diagonally, and even backward!

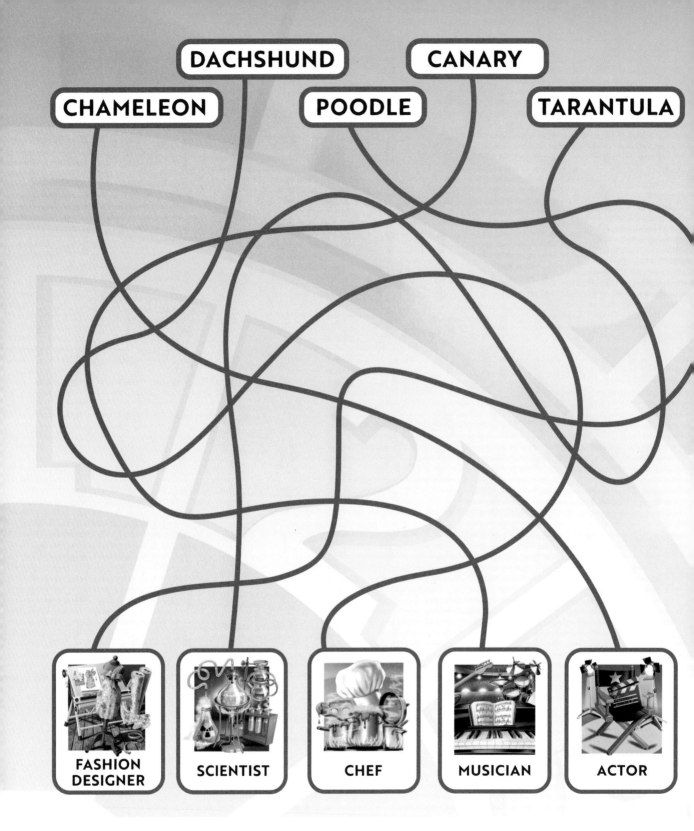

DACHSHUND

CANARY

CHAMELEON

POODLE

TARANTULA

FASHION DESIGNER

SCIENTIST

CHEF

MUSICIAN

ACTOR

WHOSE PET IS THIS?

Can you guess who owns each of these precious pets?
Follow the tangled lines and find out!

TO MY FUTURE SELF . . .

You've written a letter to your future self. But don't read the letter just yet! Fill in the blanks first, using the prompts under the blanks. You can use words from the word bank, if you like. When you're done filling in the blanks, enjoy reading your letter!

HERE ARE SOME WORDS YOU CAN USE:

NOUNS	ADJECTIVES	VERBS
bowl	clean	carry
lasagna	fiery	roll
hacky sack	shallow	fly
banana	hot	burp
actor	incredible	ski

Dear Future Me,

By the time you read this letter, you will be _____ years old. _____!
(large number)   (sound effect)

That's _____ old! Hopefully, you will be having a(n) _____ time, making
      (adjective)   (adjective)

your _____ dreams come true. Are you _____ and _____ yet? Have you
     (another large number)   (adjective)   (adjective)

gotten the _____ _____ that you always wanted? Are you living by the _____?
           (color)   (type of car)   (noun)

WHEN YOU WROTE THIS LETTER, THESE WERE YOUR GOALS:

☐ be a professional _____ player
                     (noun)

☐ own a(n) _____
           (noun)

☐ meet _____
       (name of celebrity)

☐ master the art of _____
                    (verb ending in -ing)

☐ have a _____ named _____
         (type of animal)   (name of best friend)

Have you reached these goals? That's okay if you haven't. Like _____ always says,
                                                                (name of relative)
"There's always tomorrow!"

LIFE IS FULL OF CHOICES

What will you find in your future? Spot the items listed below.

VAN   DIPLOMA   CABIN   UMBRELLA   TEACUP   MONEY

4 19 5   21 19 15 12 17   5 10

14 19   15 24 15 8 25 11 4

A = 15	H = 6	O = 10	V = 26
B = 14	I = 25	P = 7	W = 18
C = 3	J = 13	Q = 9	X = 20
D = 12	K = 16	R = 21	Y = 17
E = 19	L = 22	S = 1	Z = 8
F = 2	M = 24	T = 5	
G = 4	N = 11	U = 23	

___ ___ ___ ___ ___

___ ___ ___

THE CODE OF LIFE

Each number represents a letter. Write down the letter for each number to reveal a motivational message!

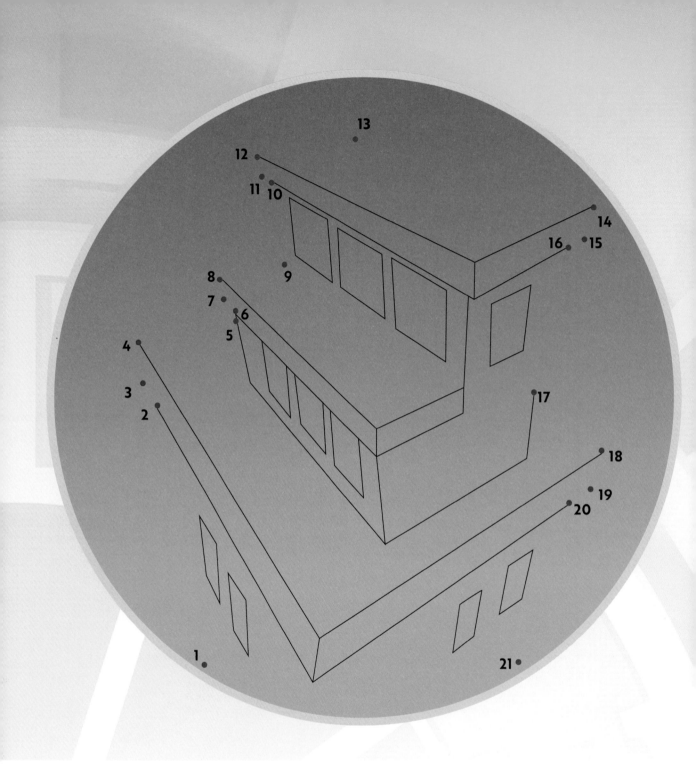

CONNECT THE DOTS

Have you ever wondered what type of home you'll live in in the future? Will it be a log home in the mountains or an apartment in the city? Connect the dots to reveal one type of home you could be living in!

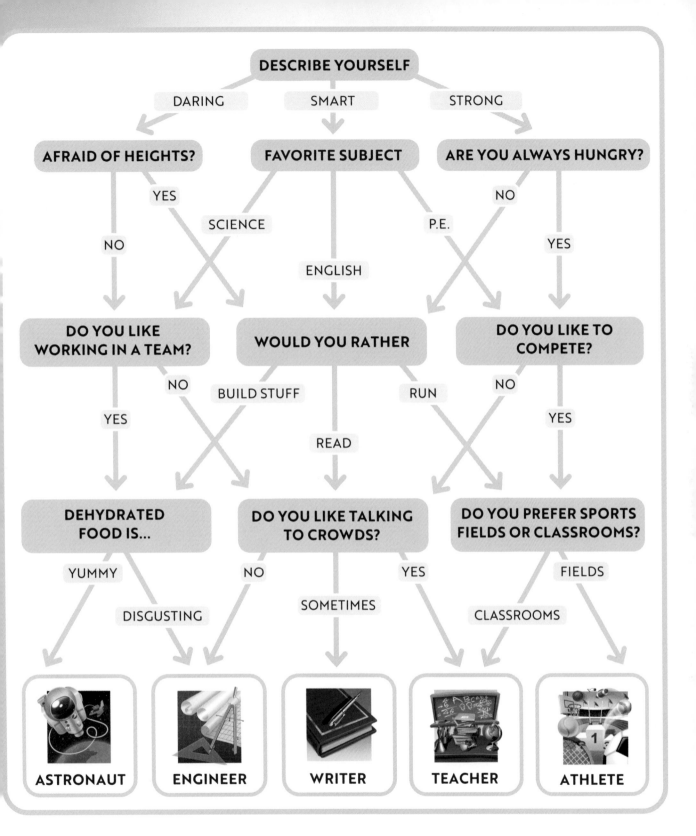

DESCRIBE YOURSELF

DARING · SMART · STRONG

AFRAID OF HEIGHTS? · **FAVORITE SUBJECT** · **ARE YOU ALWAYS HUNGRY?**

YES · SCIENCE · P.E. · NO

NO · ENGLISH · YES

DO YOU LIKE WORKING IN A TEAM? · **WOULD YOU RATHER** · **DO YOU LIKE TO COMPETE?**

NO · BUILD STUFF · RUN · NO

YES · READ · YES

DEHYDRATED FOOD IS... · **DO YOU LIKE TALKING TO CROWDS?** · **DO YOU PREFER SPORTS FIELDS OR CLASSROOMS?**

YUMMY · NO · YES · FIELDS

DISGUSTING · SOMETIMES · CLASSROOMS

ASTRONAUT · **ENGINEER** · **WRITER** · **TEACHER** · **ATHLETE**

WHEN I GROW UP . . .

What will you be when you grow up?
Take this easy quiz to find out!

MONOPOLY

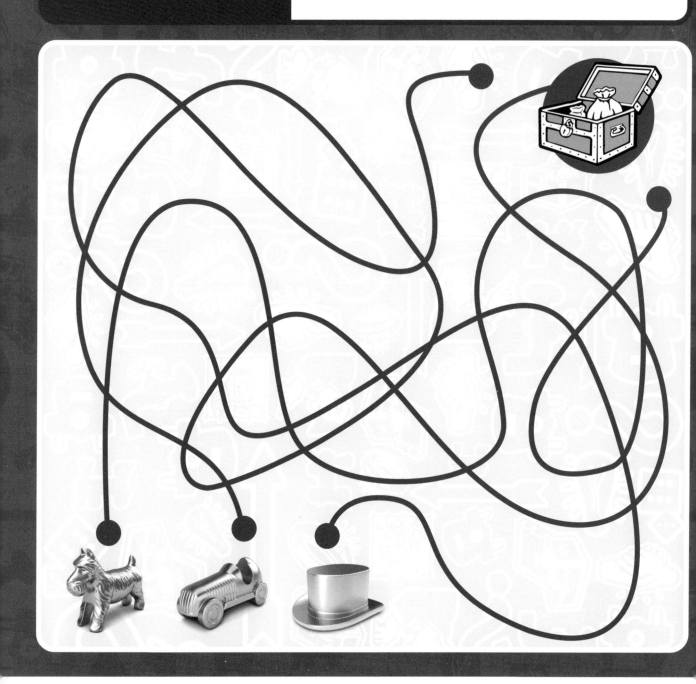

A TANGLED CLIMB

Which Monopoly token will make
it to the Community Chest first?

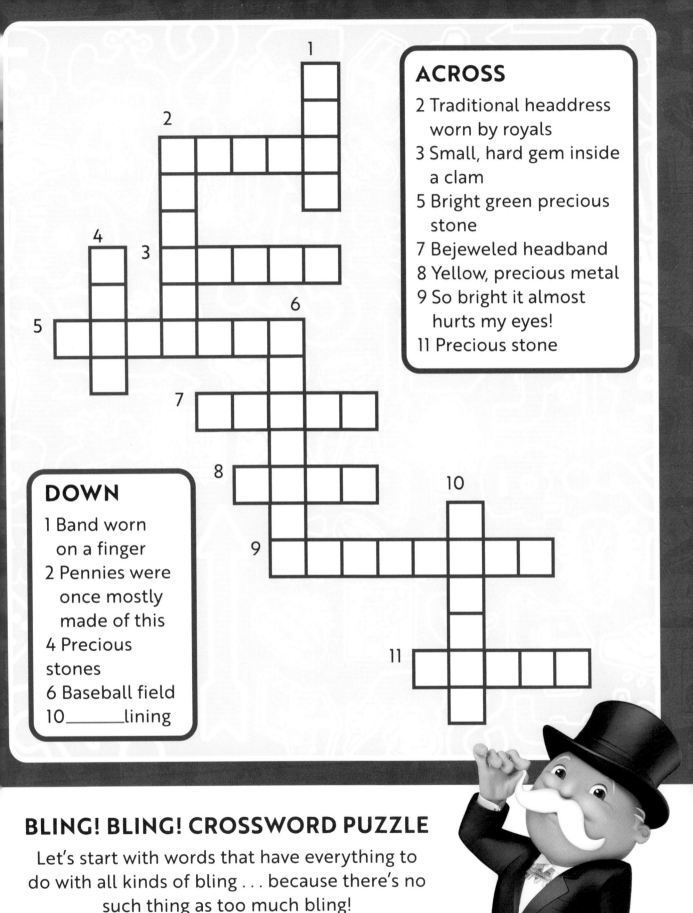

ACROSS

2 Traditional headdress worn by royals
3 Small, hard gem inside a clam
5 Bright green precious stone
7 Bejeweled headband
8 Yellow, precious metal
9 So bright it almost hurts my eyes!
11 Precious stone

DOWN

1 Band worn on a finger
2 Pennies were once mostly made of this
4 Precious stones
6 Baseball field
10 _____lining

BLING! BLING! CROSSWORD PUZZLE

Let's start with words that have everything to do with all kinds of bling . . . because there's no such thing as too much bling!

BRING ME THE RING!

Can you spot the ring?

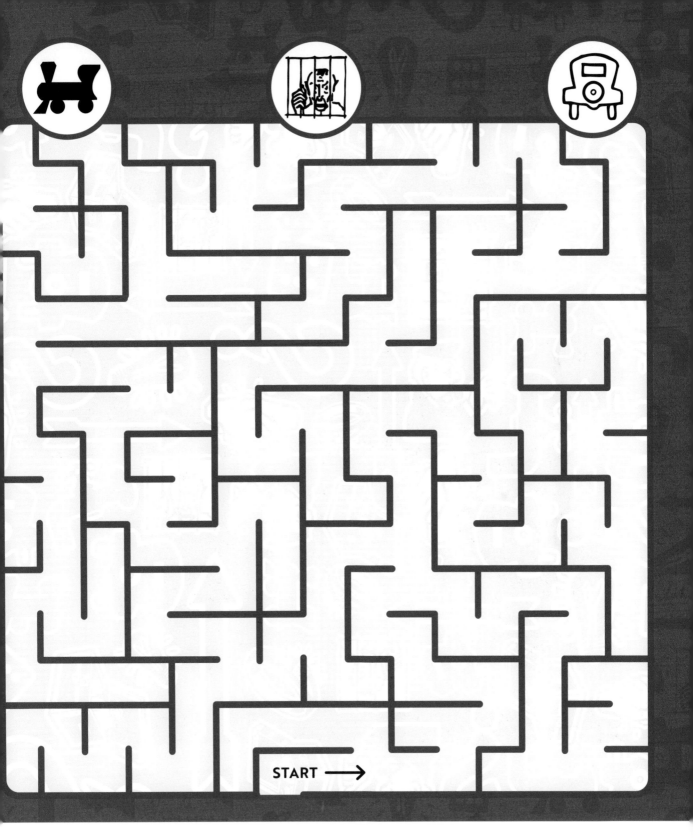

MONOPOLY MAZE

Will you go to jail, get Free Parking, or own the B&O Railroad?
Solve the maze and find out. Remember, big rewards require big risk!

SPOT THE DIFFERENCES

Stop! Do not pass GO until you spot the five differences between these two pictures!

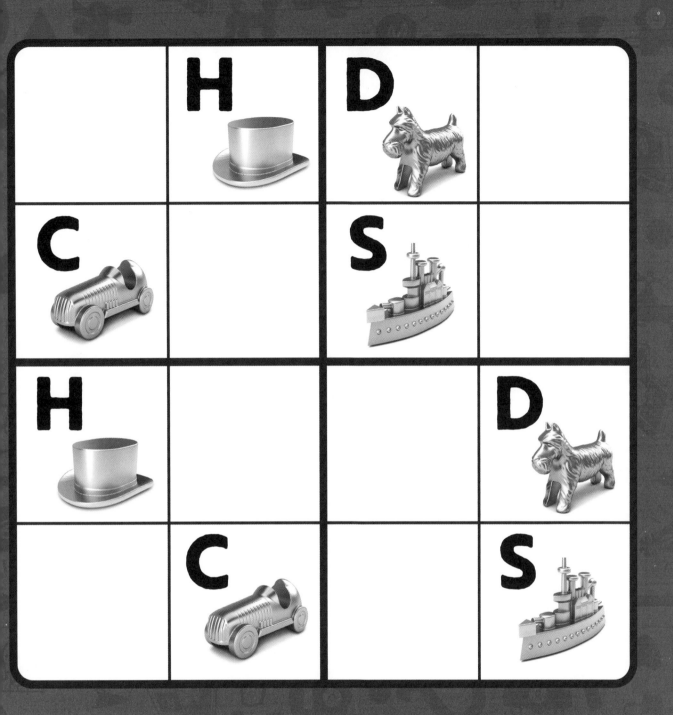

MONOPOLY SUDOKU

Fill in the grid so that each column, row, and box has one of each letter or draw in the correct token.

D H C S

ILLINOIS AVENUE

$$18 + \boxed{} \over 76$$

READING RAILROAD

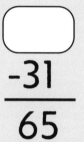

$$\boxed{} - 31 \over 65$$

WATER WORKS

$$28 + 74 \over \boxed{}$$

BOARDWALK

$$52 - \boxed{} \over 26$$

OWN IT ALL!

Figure out the missing numbers on each of these properties, and they are yours!

CONNECT THE DOTS

"Let your inner mogul shine!"

Do you pay attention to details? Are you creative? Do you like to solve problems? If you answered "yes" to all of these questions, you just might be able to solve the mysteries in this section!

G S V   Y F G O V I
W R W   R G!

A = Z	H = S	O = L	V = E
B = Y	I = R	P = K	W = D
C = X	J = Q	Q = J	X = C
D = W	K = P	R = I	Y = B
E = V	L = O	S = H	Z = A
F = U	M = N	T = G	
G = T	N = M	U = F	

__ __ __   __ __ __ __ __ __

__ __ __   __ __ !

MYSTERY MESSAGE

You received a coded message! Unscramble the letters using the key to reveal the mysterious message!

PROFESSOR PLUM

MISS SCARLET

COLONEL MUSTARD

MR. GREEN

DR. ORCHID

MRS. PEACOCK

I SPY . . . DIFFERENCES!

Test your observation skills and figure out the five
differences between these two pictures.

WHO ATE THE LAST PIECE OF CAKE?

Dr. Orchid had a weird mystery to solve last night. But don't read about it just yet! Fill in the blanks first. You can use words from the word bank to help. When you're done filling in the blanks, enjoy reading the mystery!

HERE ARE SOME WORDS YOU CAN USE:

CLUE WEAPON		CLUE MANSION ROOM	
wrench	candlestick	library	ballroom
rope	revolver	study	dining room
lead pipe	dagger	kitchen	hall

I couldn't believe what I saw: What was left on the cake plate was nothing

but _____ of crumbs! I had served each of my five guests a slice
      (small number)

of _____'s _____ cake. It had _____ , _____ , topped
   (name of relative)   (sound effect)   (type of food)   (type of sweet food)

with _____ icing. It smelled just like _____ . With my _____ , I made an
      (a color)   (something smelly)   (Clue weapon)

effort to cut equal-sized slices from the huge cake and left enough in case anyone

wanted seconds or thirds. So, you can imagine my surprise when I went back into

the _____ and found that there was nothing left! I didn't even get to have
    (room in the Clue mansion)

any! I was about to barge back into the _____ to get someone to confess
                                        (room in the Clue mansion)

when— _____ !—I slipped on some icing and fell on my _____ ! That's when I
       (sound effect)   (body part)

noticed a trail of cake crumbs as long as a _____ leading to the _____ .
                                            (Clue weapon)   (room in the Clue mansion)

I rushed out and found _____ , my beloved _____ , with icing on
                       (a friend's name)   (type of pet)

its _____ , looking like a sad _____ !
   (a body part)   (cartoon character)

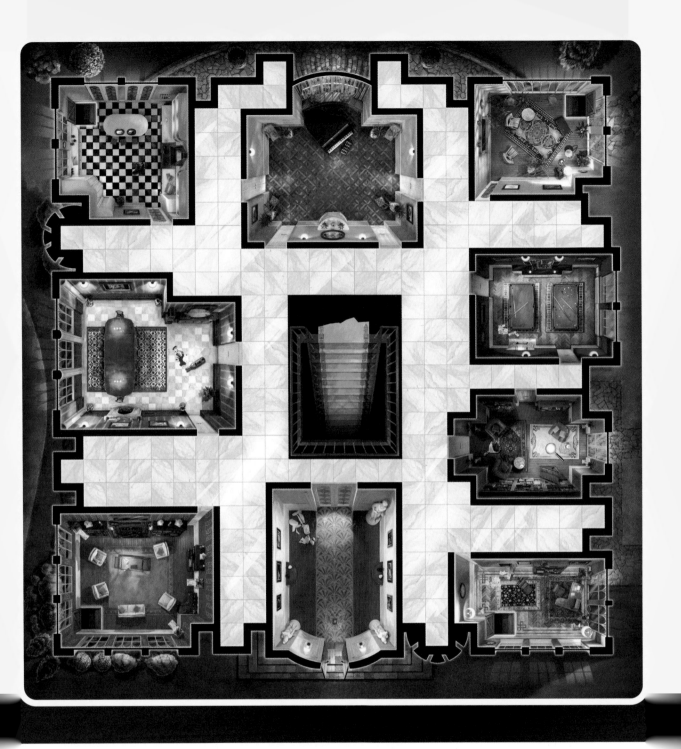

WHERE IS IT?

A suspect has left their magnifying glass in one of the rooms at the mansio Finding the magnifying glass—and figuring out whose fingerprints are on it would mean solving the mystery! Can you locate where it is on the map of the mansion . . . before anyone else does?

```
E P O R L H V H Q B P U Y B M
E Y D U T S L I B R A R Y A O
L E V R R L D C D G O L V L O
O P D H E X L A E T B F C L R
U I G I G V G A A L A E K R D
N P E J N G L V H O L C P O R
G D L O E I R O Q T I A J O A
E A O R M E N K V T E V R M I
G E C A S P I G S E R B Q X L
U L Z N S T K E R V R H D S L
K N O I C V L E L O M M O X I
H C E H F D F G V G O G P R B
H E E A N W R E N C H M O S P
E N M A F C H A R R D L Y G N
N Z C T E R T R U H C G Z A N
```

DINING ROOM   HALL   CELLAR   REVOLVER
LOUNGE   BILLIARD ROOM   BALLROOM   LEAD PIPE
KITCHEN   CONSERVATORY   DAGGER   CANDLESTICK
STUDY   LIBRARY   ROPE   WRENCH

CLUE WORD SEARCH

Uncover the 15 words related to the rooms and
weapons used in the game. You can find the words in all
directions: across, down, diagonally, and even backward!

Where to dance the night away

B __ **L L** ⭕ __ __ __

Where to make tasty treats

K ⭕ __ __ __ __ __

What a lasso is made of

__ ⭕ __ __

Where to read and work

__ **T U** ⭕ __

What is used to hold a candle

⭕ __ **N** __ __ **E** __ __ __ __ __

What to use to tighten a pipe

__ __ __ __ **C** ⭕

WRITE EACH LETTER IN THE CIRCLES HERE.

WHO SOLVED THE MYSTERY? UNSCRAMBLE THE LETTERS.

WHO SOLVED IT?

Fill in the answers to the puzzle and unscramble the letters that land in the circles. They will spell out the name of the person who solved the mystery!

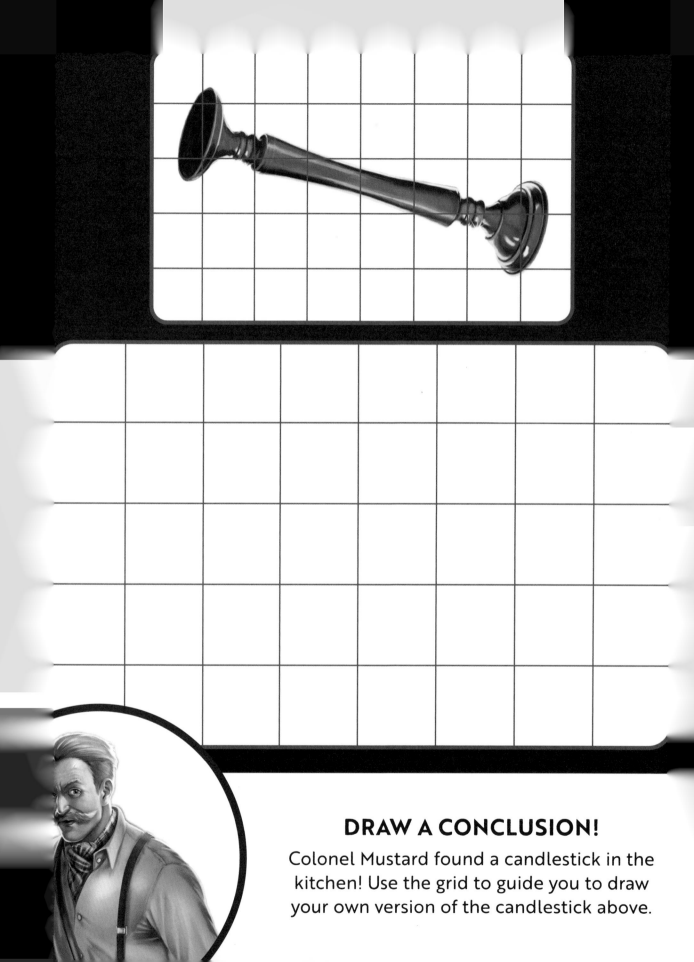

DRAW A CONCLUSION!

Colonel Mustard found a candlestick in the kitchen! Use the grid to guide you to draw your own version of the candlestick above.

IT'S A MYSTERY!

Professor Plum needs your help to find one last piece of
evidence that will wrap up the mystery at the local hotel.
Follow the tangled lines to figure out just what it is!

OPERATION

Is there a doctor in the house?
It's time to operate!

CONNECT THE DOTS!

Dr. Pearl Patience just got a new patient! Connect the dots to reveal who just arrived.

```
T E D Y F I S B I R
R T L C H T X R P I
A L N K O W E N U A
E W Y M C V G O P H
H L A K I U L X I V
K C P L O J N N L R
H N H P F X O K U A
E Y E L A S H J B R
C D N E T S X Z C I
T X Y R C H M Z F O
R E I N W A H A R K
K L W U X R P D D W
E N O B T S I R W A
```

STOMACH	HEART	KNEECAP	WRIST BONE
RIBS	LIVER	PUPIL	ADAM'S APPLE
KNUCKLE	EYELASH	NOSTRIL	HAIR

BODY PARTS WORD SEARCH

Look for the 12 body parts in the word bank. You can
find the words in all directions in the word search:
across, down, diagonally, and even backward!

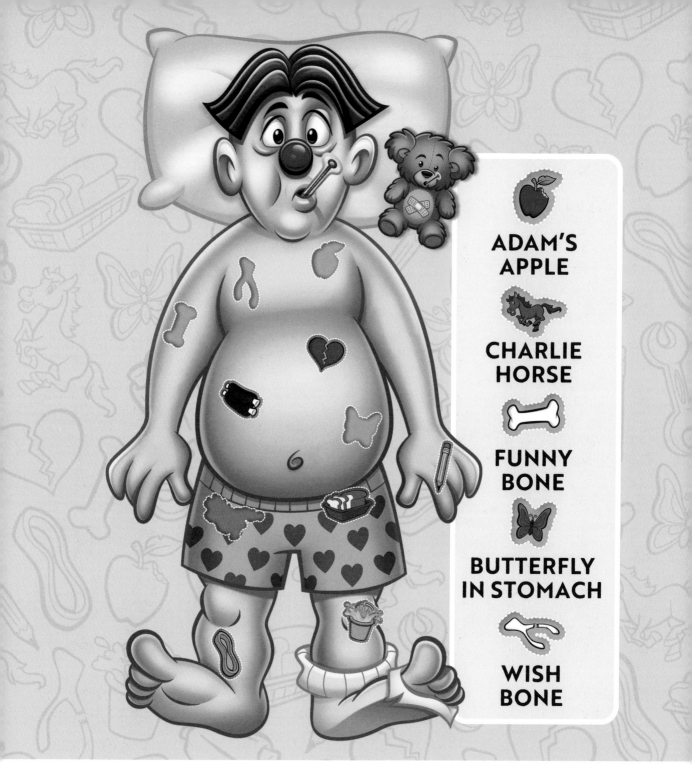

ADAM'S APPLE

CHARLIE HORSE

FUNNY BONE

BUTTERFLY IN STOMACH

WISH BONE

WHAT'S MISSING?

Something strange is happening to Cavity Sam. He is missing some body parts . . . but seems to have a few new ones! Can you draw them in, so the doctor can take a better look? Use the word bank to help you fill in the gaps!

START

DOCTOR, DOCTOR!

Quick, help Cavity Sam get to the hospital! Watch out for ambulances and road construction . . . but be sure to pick up three wish bones along the way!

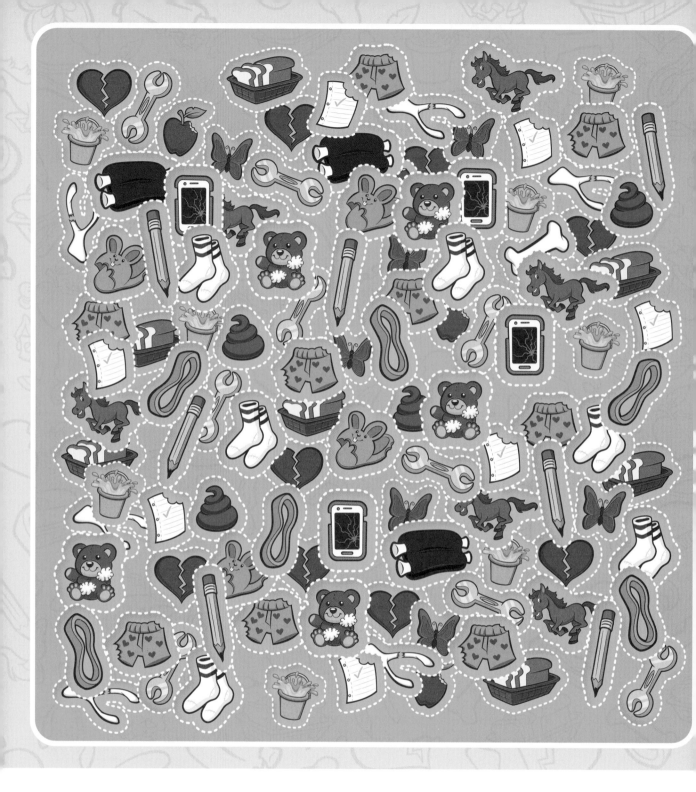

SHOW ME THE FUNNY . . . BONE!

Cavity Sam is not happy. He's lost his funny bone! Can you help him find it?

A FLUTTER OF BUTTERFLIES!

Cavity Sam must be really nervous about his upcoming
operation. Look at all the butterflies in his stomach!
Count them all . . . before they fly away!

ONE (ADJECTIVE) NIGHT AT THE HOSPITAL!

Dr. Barney Bumblelot has written a letter about why he can't show up for work today. But don't read the letter just yet! Fill in the blanks first, using the prompts under each blank line. You can use words from the word bank, if you like. When you're done filling in the blanks, enjoy reading the letter!

HERE ARE SOME WORDS YOU CAN USE:

NOUNS	ADJECTIVE	VERBS	AILMENTS
shampoo	icky	shuffle	Charlie horse
sunscreen	gloomy	wobble	brain freeze
avocado	teeny tiny	sweep	butterflies in stomach
firefly	tricky	bring	writer's cramp
hotel	curvy	spin	wrenched ankle
attic	curious		water on the knee

Dear Chief of Medicine,

Yesterday was a(n) _____ night at the hospital! Maybe there was a(n) _____ moon
(adjective) (adjective)

or something, but this is all that happened: First _____ _____ in with
(name of a friend) (past tense verb)

a(n) _____ _____ named _____. The horse had a(n) _____, so
(adjective) (animal) (name of pet) (ailment)

we _____ its _____ right away. Then _____ _____ in with
(past tense verb) (body part) (name of relative) (past tense verb)

a(n) _____, so we tossed the _____ and started to _____ the _____. But just
(ailment) (noun) (verb) (body part)

as we did that, the lights went out! We had to bring out the _____ to see what we
(plural noun)

were doing. It was _____! In the dark, Dr. _____ reached for a(n) _____ to fix
(adjective) (vegetable) (noun)

the _____, Nurse _____ moved a(n) _____ because _____ had _____,
(ailment) (place) (noun) (name) (ailment)

and I stood on a(n) _____ to take a better look at _____'s _____. I fell
(noun) (name of friend) (ailment)

down and twisted my _____! So, this is why I'm not getting out of bed today.
(body part)

Sincerely,

Dr. Barney Bumblelot

ALMOST TWINS

These two pictures of Cavity Sam look alike . . .
except for five differences. Can you spot them?

 **Trivial Pursuit**

NOONDL ⟶ _ O _ _ O _

TOOKY ⟶ T _ _ Y _

TWOTAO ⟶ _ T T _ _ _

ACORI ⟶ C A _ _ _

SCARAAC ⟶ _ A R _ _ A _

KARTAAJ ⟶ J _ K _ _ T _

RIBLEN ⟶ _ _ R _ _ N

GIEBJIN ⟶ B _ _ J _ _ _

RIDDAM ⟶ M _ _ R _ _

OLUSE ⟶ S E _ U _

NIBLUD ⟶ _ U _ _ I N

MIXED-UP CAPITALS

The capital of France is Spria! Spria? You mean Paris! Unscramble the letters to find the names of these other capitals of the world.

```
K G V Z R G C G Q P T S
U C A Q E C N R R B E N
H E A P W I D E O A K O
K O G R M O C B B S C W
P A C M T C S A F K I B
S K I K O L D S Y E R O
K W X S E M E A K T C A
S P W D I Y R L L B M R
X T Y N Y M P Q V A E D
T C T R O W I N G L E I
U O E T A R A K C L Z N
N B A S E B A L L U U G
```

SOCCER	BADMINTON	SWIMMING
BASEBALL	KARATE	ROWING
HOCKEY	TRACK	SNOWBOARDING
BASKETBALL	CRICKET	BOBSLED

LET'S PLAY!

Look for the 12 sports in the word bank. You can
find the words in all directions in the word search:
across, down, diagonally, and even backward!

NATURE ADVENTURE

Going on a hike is often fun and informative. Just be sure to stay on the right path!

NOTE: Don't read the story yet! Fill in the blanks first, using the prompts under each blank line. You can use words from the word bank, if you like. When you're done filling in the blanks, enjoy reading your hilarious story!

HERE ARE SOME WORDS YOU CAN USE:

NOUNS		ADJECTIVE	
couch	flute	rocky	stinky
cupcake	cushion	pointy	ridiculous
highlighter	rattle	great	creepy
clock	snail	messy	hairy

Dear _____ ,
　　　　　(name of relative)

You won't believe what happened to me on my trip to _____ Park! First, let
　　　　　　　　　　　　　　　　　　　　　　　　　　　(sound)

me just say that it was_____and _____! So _____ , _____ ,
　　　　　　　　　　　　　((adjective)　　　(adjective)　　　(name of friend)　　(name of another friend)

and _____ took the _____ _____ path up to _____ mountain. We
　　(name of pet)　　　　　(adjective)　(name of TV show)　　　(name of grocery store)

came across _____ , _____ , and _____ . We saw a(n) _____ _____ and
　　　　　　(name of bugs)　(name of reptiles)　(plural noun)　　　　　(color)　(animal)

many _____ . We were so _____ we didn't notice that we had gone the wrong
　　　(plural noun)　　　　　　(adjective)

way, . . . and we were lost! Then _____ fell and bumped her _____ on
　　　　　　　　　　　　　　　　　(name of same friend)　　　　　　　　　(body part)

a(n) _____ . After walking around in circles for _____ hours, we heard a _____ . It
　　(noun)　　　　　　　　　　　　　　　　　(large number)　　　　　　　　(sound)

was Ms. _____ , the park ranger! She said she followed the trail of _____ that one
　　　(name of animal)　　　　　　　　　　　　　　　　　　　　　(noun)

of us must have accidentally created. It was a(n) _____ thing she found us because it
　　　　　　　　　　　　　　　　　　　　(adjective)

started raining _____ as soon as we got back to the start of the trail. You know this
　　　　　　　(plural noun)

wouldn't have happened if you were there. So, you're coming with us next time!

Love,

_____
(Your name)

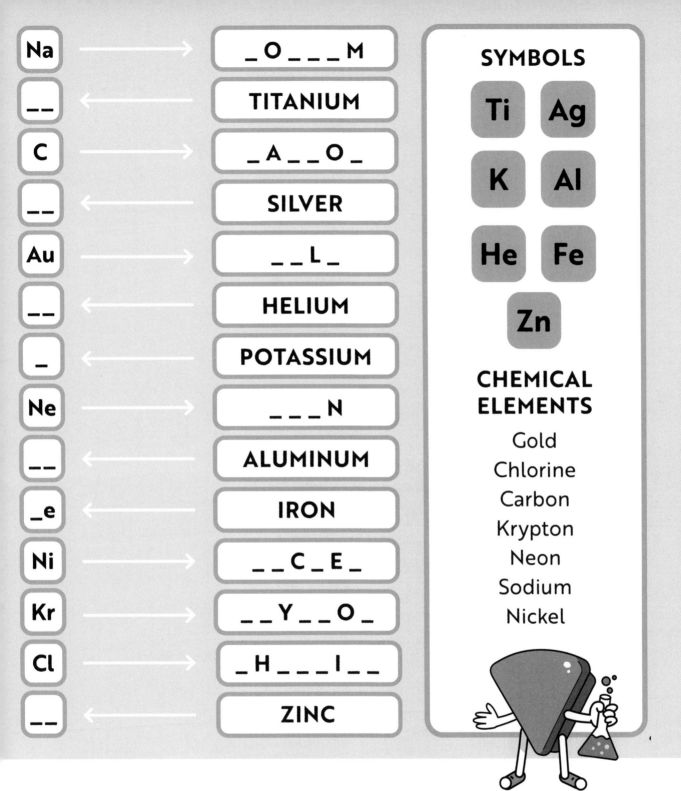

Symbol		Element name
Na	→	_ O _ _ _ M
_ _	←	TITANIUM
C	↔	_ A _ _ O _
_ _	←	SILVER
Au	→	_ _ L _
_ _	←	HELIUM
_	←	POTASSIUM
Ne	→	_ _ _ N
_ _	←	ALUMINUM
_e	←	IRON
Ni	→	_ _ C _ E _
Kr	→	_ _ Y _ _ O _
Cl	→	_ H _ _ _ I _ _
_ _	←	ZINC

SYMBOLS

Ti Ag

K Al

He Fe

Zn

CHEMICAL ELEMENTS

Gold
Chlorine
Carbon
Krypton
Neon
Sodium
Nickel

CHEMICAL ATTRACTION

Chemical elements are represented by letter symbols, such as O for oxygen or H for hydrogen. Fill in the blanks on this table, matching the symbols to the correct chemical elements. Use the list of symbols and chemical elements to help!

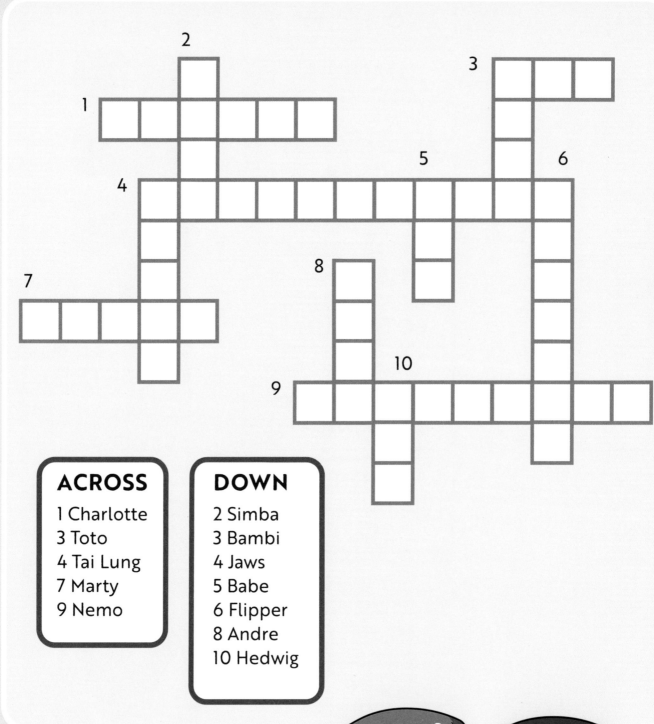

ACROSS
1 Charlotte
3 Toto
4 Tai Lung
7 Marty
9 Nemo

DOWN
2 Simba
3 Bambi
4 Jaws
5 Babe
6 Flipper
8 Andre
10 Hedwig

ANIMALS AT THE MOVIES

What type of animals are these movie characters?

HALF A MASTERPIECE

More than 500 years ago, Leonardo da Vinci painted the masterpiece
known as the *Mona Lisa*. Millions of people have seen this work of art,
and now you get to draw the other half of this famous portrait!

INVENTIONS	INVENTORS
BASKETBALL	FREDERICK MCKINLEY JONES
AUTOMATIC ELEVATOR DOORS	CAI LUN
WINDSHIELD WIPERS	MELITTA BENTZ
TELEPHONE	ALEXANDER GRAHAM BELL
CALCULATOR	BLAISE PASCAL
LIGHT BULB	JAMES NAISMITH
PAPER BAG	ALEXANDER MILES
COFFEE FILTER	MARY ANDERSON
REFRIGERATED TRUCK	MARGARET KNIGHT
PAPER	THOMAS EDISON

WHO CAME UP WITH THAT?

Necessity is the mother of invention, but who are the parents of these everyday items? Draw a line between these inventions and their inventors and see if you can guess: *Who came up with that?*

WORDS IN WORDS

Can you make 10 words from the words TRIVIAL PURSUIT?
Challenge yourself: No words with less than three letters, please!

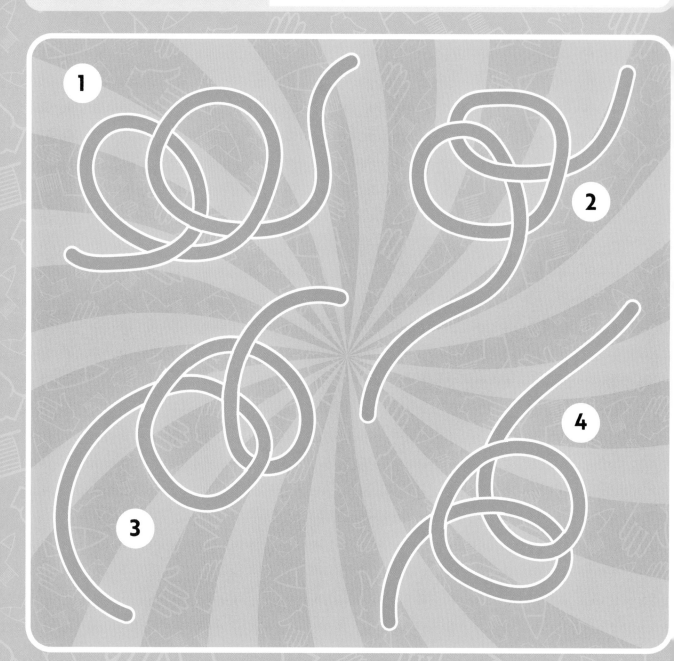

A KNOTTY PROBLEM

Only one of these strings will form a knot
when it is pulled. Which one is it?

A Y F S U J H J X
T Z E J W A H S G
D H D L N U G T R
X E G D L A K R E
R D S I I O K E E
N E X Y R T W T N
T N F R B F R S T
B L U E T E X I U
S T O O F L P W B
A Q K A Z X W T R
B X F S O K M V F

TWISTER   YELLOW   FOOT
RED   GREEN   RIGHT
BLUE   HAND   LEFT

WINDY WORDS

Look for the nine twisting words in the word search. You can find the words in all directions in the word search: across, down, diagonally, and backward!

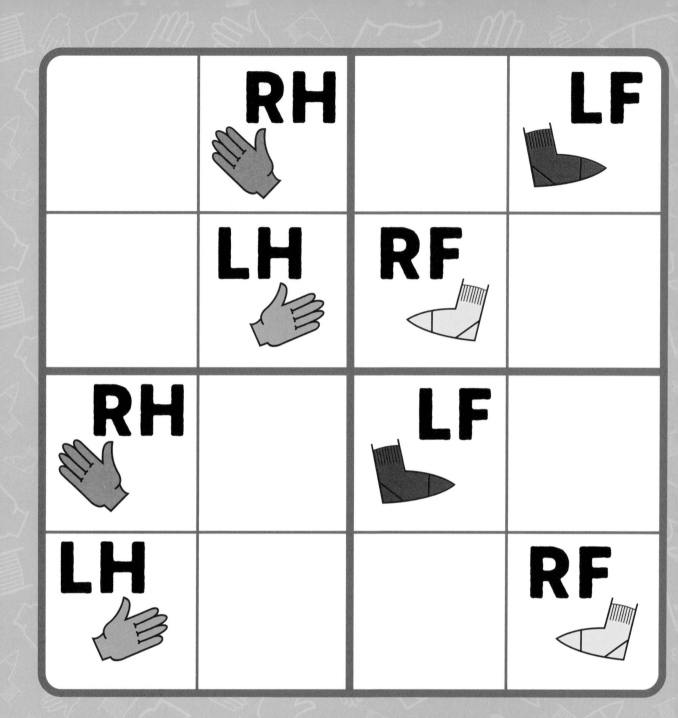

TWISTER SUDOKU

Fill in the grid so that each column, row, and box has one of each group of letters and draw in the correct hand or foot. Color them in for added fun!

NO SOCKS!	CHANDELIER
GET A GRIP	BIGFOOT
FANCY LIGHTING	SECONDHAND
YETI	FOOTPRINTS
USED	BAREFOOT
TRACKS	HANDLE
DO AS YOU PLEASE	HANDSOME
GOOD LOOKING	MERCHANDISE
A FRIENDLY GESTURE	FOOTLOOSE
GOODS	SUREFOOTED
HAPPENING OR STARTING TO HAPPEN	HANDSHAKE
CONFIDENT	AFOOT

GIVE ME A HAND . . . OR A FOOT!

Each word on the right side contains the letters "hand" or "foot." On the left are clues that need to be matched to the words on the right. Draw a line to match the related words in each column.

```
S K T S I R S D T U F E
T L H I A K E U H O O D
N X R D X R R V R Q P I
E R O E B N O W O D P S
C W U W Y L A U N H O N
A Y G A I R W I N G S I
J B H Y D C H P V D I M
D Z O S B E Y O N D T Q
A I V V B E W M H R E F
K X N V E R E D N U A U
Q F D O D M S S O R C A
C L O C K W I S E D M D
```

AROUND	OVER	ABOVE	CLOCKWISE
SIDEWAYS	INSIDE	OPPOSITE	THROUGH
FORWARD	BEHIND	ACROSS	TURN
UNDER	BEYOND	ADJACENT	

WHICH WAY? WORD SEARCH

Look for the 15 direction-themed words in the word search, but don't get turned around! You can find the words in all directions in the word search: across, down, diagonally, and even backward!

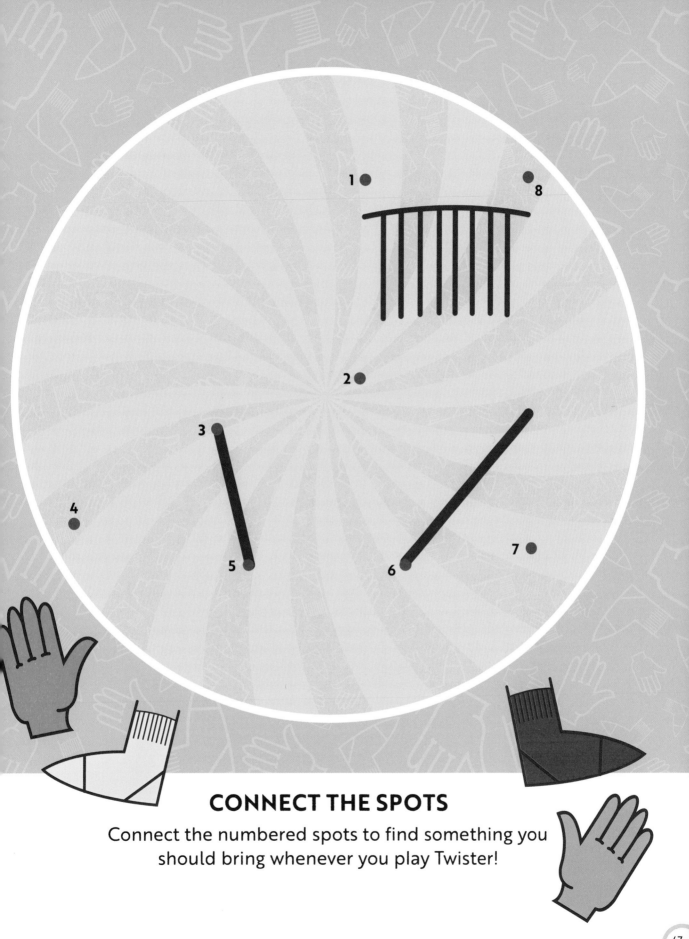

CONNECT THE SPOTS

Connect the numbered spots to find something you should bring whenever you play Twister!

THREE TONGUE TWISTERS

A = 26	E = 22	I = 18	M = 14	Q = 3	U = 7	Y = 11
B = 25	F = 21	J = 17	N = 13	R = 4	V = 8	Z = 12
C = 24	G = 20	K = 16	O = 1	S = 5	W = 9	
D = 23	H = 19	L = 15	P = 2	T = 6	X = 10	

21 4 22 5 19 / 21 4 18 22 23 / 21 18 5 19, 21 18 5 19
21 4 22 5 19 / 21 4 18 22 23, 21 4 18 22 23 / 21 18 5 19
21 4 22 5 19, 21 18 5 19 / 21 4 18 22 23 / 21 4 22 5 19

2 1 2 2 11 / 2 7 6 / 26 / 24 7 2 / 1 21
2 4 1 2 22 4 / 24 1 21 21 22 22 / 18 13 / 26
24 1 2 2 22 4 / 24 1 21 21 22 22 / 24 7 2

24 4 18 5 2 / 24 4 7 5 6 5 / 24 4 26 24 16 15 22,
24 4 18 5 2 / 24 4 7 5 6 5 / 24 4 7 13 24 19,
24 4 18 5 2 11 / 24 4 26 24 16 15 11 / 24 4 7 5 6 5,
24 4 7 13 24 19 / 24 4 7 13 24 19 / 24 4 7 13 24 19

SECRET TONGUE TWISTERS

Each number represents a letter. Write down the letter for each number to crack the code and reveal each tongue twister. Then say the tongue twister three times fast!

GIVE ME A HAND . . . OR A FOOT!

Follow the line to determine which body part should be placed on red.

Game on! It's 4 for the win!

	3	4	
4			2
1			3
	2	1	

CONNECT4 SUDOKU

Fill in the grid so that each column, row, and box
has the numbers 1 through 4 in them.

```
R  A  L  P  I  L  I  T  F
Z  V  J  D  A  D  D  C  O
F  C  T  Z  A  Q  T  E  U
G  O  K  N  X  L  T  N  R
M  I  U  L  W  C  X  N  J
P  B  M  R  E  U  G  O  K
T  E  E  N  O  K  M  C  W
J  C  N  R  F  D  B  C  Z
G  O  E  O  R  U  O  F  B
C  I  U  N  S  P  O  E  E
E  R  X  K  N  R  T  F  I
T  E  W  G  Q  O  U  N  H
Y  C  O  N  N  E  C  T  W
```

WORD SEARCH

The words "Connect" and "Four" appear
four times. Find all of them!

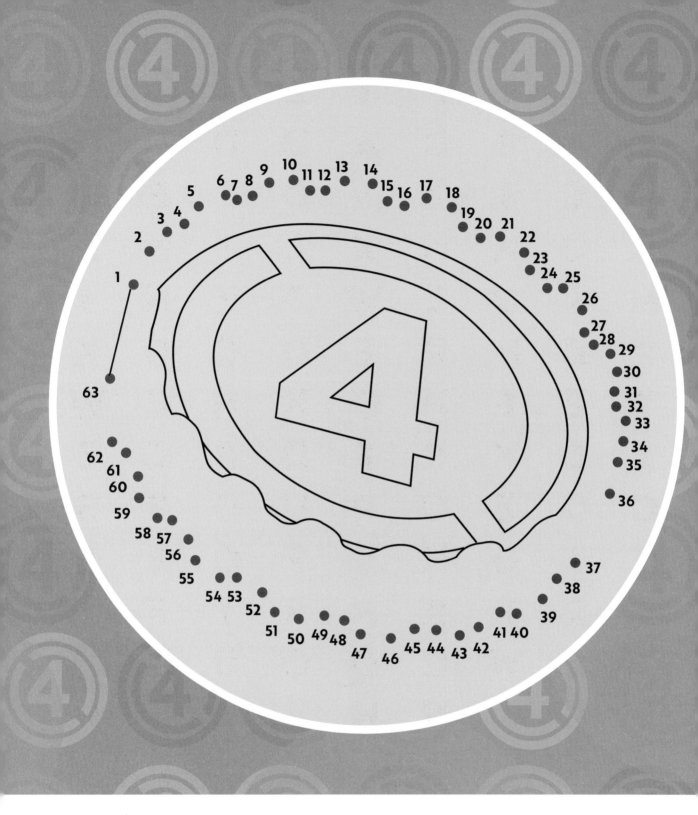

CONNECT THE DOTS

Connect the dots to reveal what you need "4 the win"!

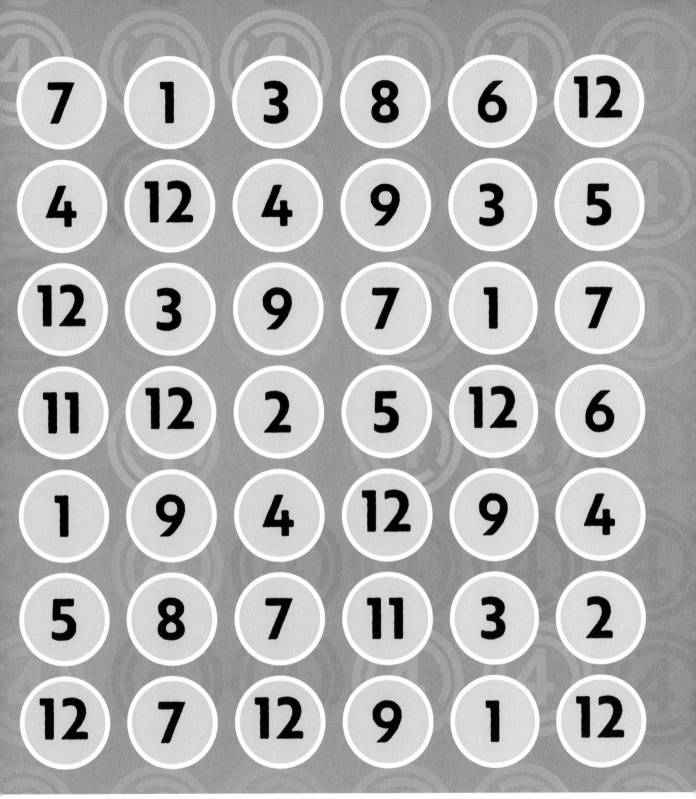

7	1	3	8	6	12
4	12	4	9	3	5
12	3	9	7	1	7
11	12	2	5	12	6
1	9	4	12	9	4
5	8	7	11	3	2
12	7	12	9	1	12

ADD THEM UP!

Grab two dice and roll them to play. Add up the numbers on the dice and color in the sum on this page. First player to get four in a row wins!

PLAY WITH A FRIEND!

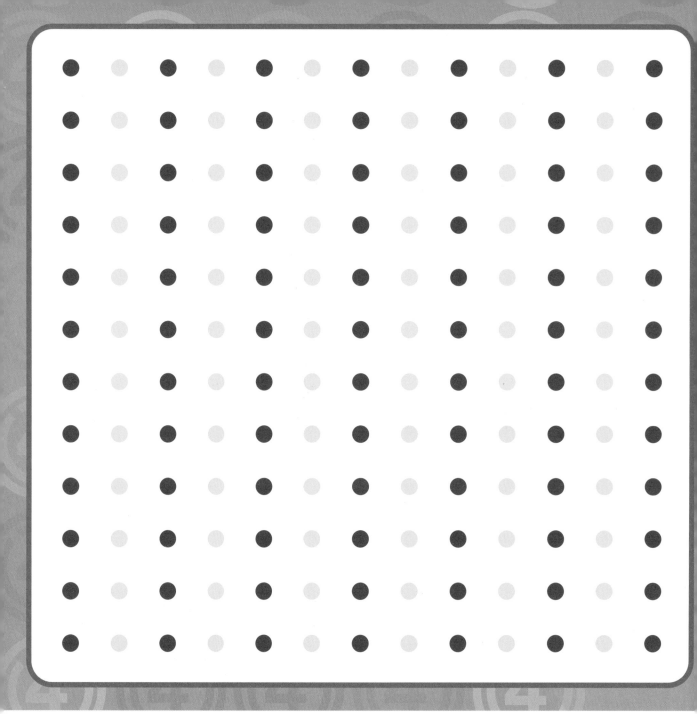

WHO'S THE SQUAREST ONE OF ALL?

Square off with a friend—or two!—to make as many squares as possible on this grid.

HOW TO PLAY: TAKE TURNS CONNECTING DOTS TO MAKE SQUARES. EACH CONNECTING LINE IS A TURN. THE PERSON WHO CLOSES UP EACH SQUARE PUTS THEIR INITIALS IN THE SQUARE.

When all the dots are connected, count up the number of squares with your initials. The one with most squares wins!

PLAY WITH A FRIEND!

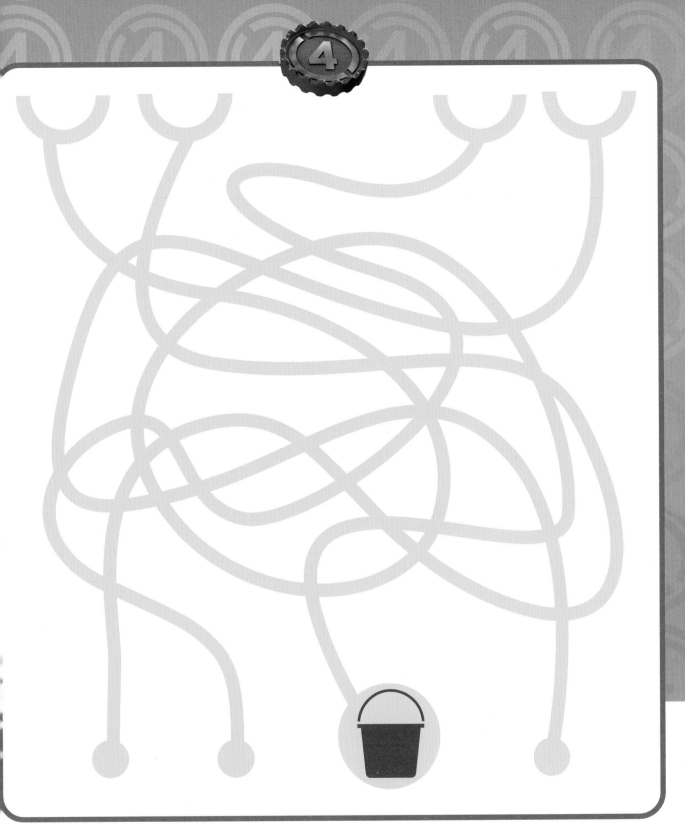

COIN DROP!

Drop your coin into the bucket! But which pipe will make the right connection with the bucket?

PLAY TO WIN!

Each of these games need just one more move to win. You are playing red. Where would you drop in the last disc?

LEONARDO, RAPHAEL, DONATELLO, MICHELANGELO	THE BEATLES
JOHN, PAUL, GEORGE, AND RINGO	SUITS IN A CARD DECK
NORTH, SOUTH, EAST, WEST	SEASONS
SPRING, SUMMER, FALL, WINTER	COMPASS POINTS
WATER, EARTH, FIRE, AIR	TEENAGE MUTANT NINJA TURTLES
SPADES, CLUBS, HEARTS, DIAMONDS	FANTASTIC FOUR
HUMAN TORCH, INVISIBLE WOMAN, MR. FANTASTIC, THE THING	CLASSICAL ELEMENTS

CONNECT THE FOURS

Some people say the best things come in fours. Can you match the clues of four things on the left to the list on the right?

Guess who likes sports, animals, reading, traveling, and more? That's right! It's the Guess Who? crew. Everyone is always welcome to join this cheery group for fun and games anytime!

DRAWING JORDAN

When he's not busy meeting sports stars or skateboarding, Jordan loves to draw! Just for fun, he's drawn in half his face. Can you fill in the other half?

SOMETHING'S DIFFERENT ABOUT AMY

Amy loves a good prank! Can you spot five differences between
these two pictures of Amy, or will you fall for her prank?

THIS PERSON:

- ? HAS SHORT HAIR
- ? DOESN'T WEAR A HAT
- ? DOESN'T HAVE A BEARD
- ? WEARS GLASSES
- ? ALWAYS WEARS SOMETHING PURPLE

WHO ARE YOU LOOKING FOR, SOFIA?

Sofia is looking for her friend to go with her to the local thrift store, and it's up to you to guess who it is! Check out the clues to find the answer.

```
R W A R J V C E C L
L A O M I X E T O B
U C T O P A L U U L
K B L I Q P L L N U
H I S K U Q O F T E
N E M L G G G P R S
Q Y U Z Z A J C Y N
F S R U B O N A I P
P M D T R E C N O C
M I C R O P H O N E
A H A R M O N Y M G
```

CELLO	GUITAR	AMP	CONCERT	POP
VIOLIN	DRUMS	COUNTRY	FLUTE	BLUES
PIANO	MICROPHONE	ROCK	HARMONY	JAZZ

SAM'S WORD SEARCH

When it comes to music, Sam is your guy! Can you find the 15 words related to music and musical instruments listed in the word bank? You can find them in all directions in the word search: across, down, diagonally, and even backward!

START ⟶

EMMA'S MAZE

Good news: Emma found a book she really likes at the library. It's a real page turner!

Bad news: She's too into her book to watch where she's going. Can you make sure she meets up with her friends safely?

Scramble		Answer
MEGILUB	→	_ _ L G _ _ _
NITZAAAN	→	T _ _ Z _ _ I _
AIRCOAT	→	C _ _ _ T _ A
PLANE	→	_ E _ A _
RATINAGEN	→	A _ G E _ T _ N _
SOLA	→	L _ _ S
UVUTANA	→	_ A _ U _ T U
YERTUK	→	_ _ R K _ _
CEEGER	→	_ R _ _ _ E
AMETALUGA	→	G _ _ T _ M _ _ _

AL'S ON VACAY!

Al loves to travel. Can you unscramble the letters to reveal the names of countries that are on his wish list?

THE CLASSIC NAVAL COMBAT GAME
BATTLESHIP

Attention, everyone! It's time to assemble and prepare for action on the high seas!

A	.-	E	.	I	..	M	--	Q	--.-	U	..-	Y	-.--
B	-...	F	..-.	J	.---	N	-.	R	.-.	V	...-	Z	--..
C	-.-.	G	--.	K	-.-	O	---	S	...	W	.--		
D	-..	H	....	L	.-..	P	.--.	T	-	X	-..-		

-- -. . .- . . -. . --- --- -...!

.-- .-- --- .. ... . -. .- -.

- ....-.

-... . .- - .-.. . ...--.!

MESSAGE FROM THE ADMIRAL!

The admiral has sent a message to the members of his fleet. Can you figure out what it is? Each symbol represents a letter. Write down the letter for each symbol to reveal the message.

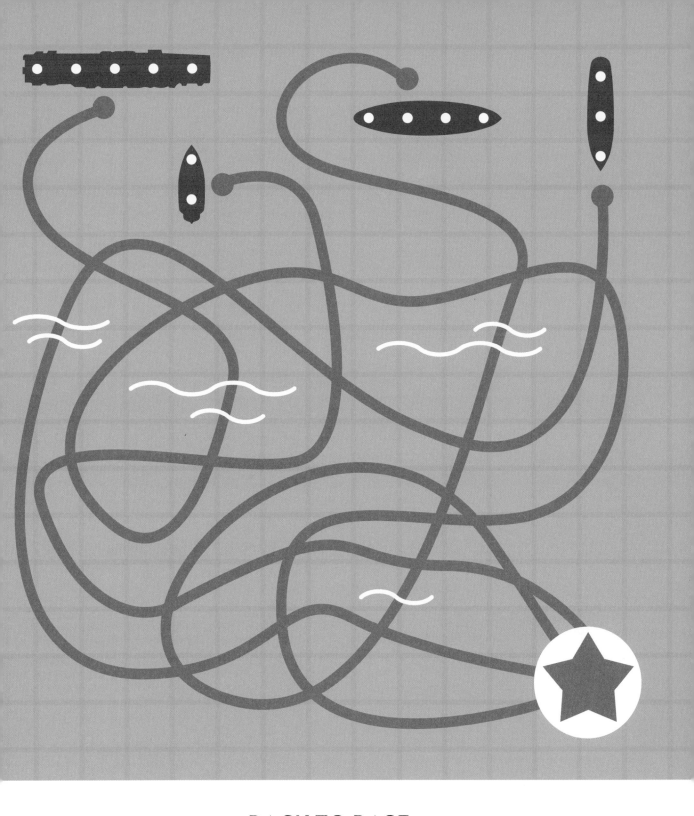

BACK TO BASE

These four vessels are racing back to the naval base, but three of the paths are blocked! Find the one clear path to find out which ship reached the naval base the quickest!

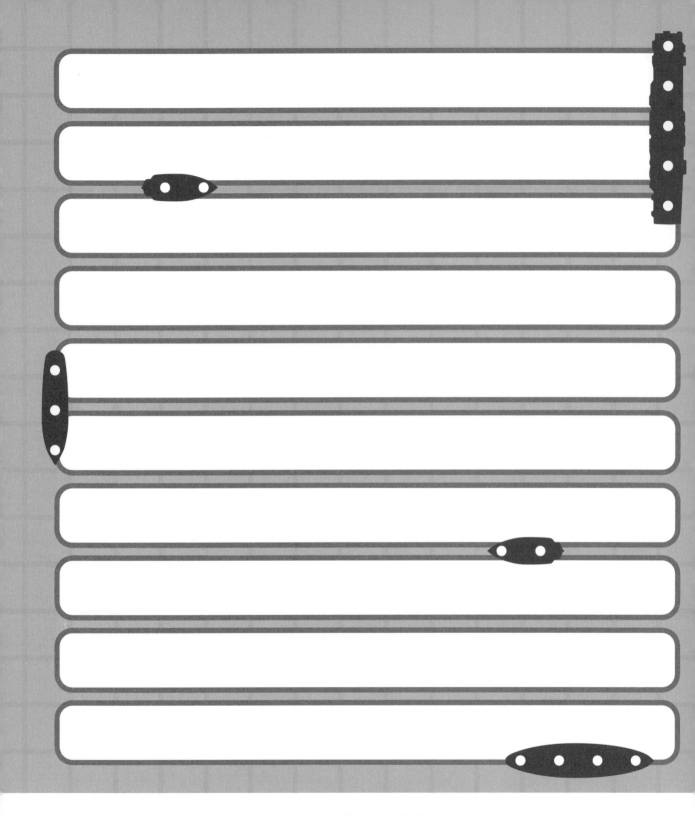

AYE, AYE, CAPTAIN!

The captain has issued an order: Make 10 words from the word **BATTLESHIP** . . . and they must be at least three letters long!

WHICH WAY TO SAFE HARBOR?

Your ship has to make it to safe harbor at
Naval Island. Watch out for the sunken
battleships and enemy ships along the way!

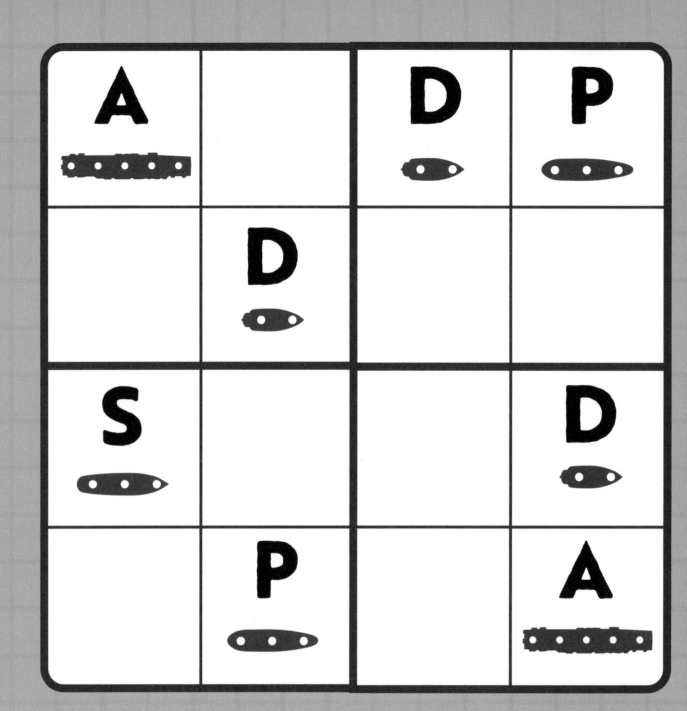

BATTLESHIP SUDOKU

Fill in the grid so that each column, row, and box has one of each letter and draw in the correct battleship!

A S P D

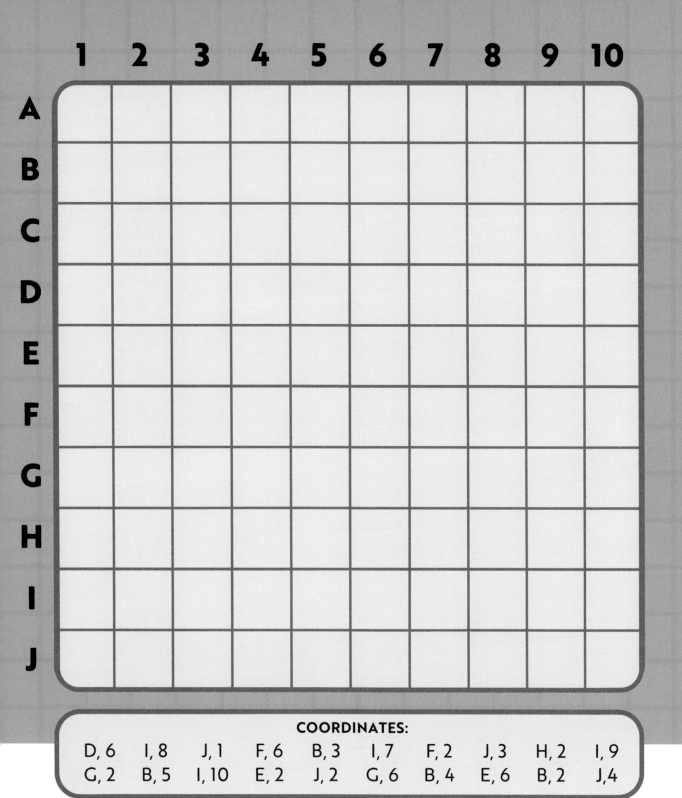

	1	2	3	4	5	6	7	8	9	10
A										
B										
C										
D										
E										
F										
G										
H										
I										
J										

COORDINATES:

| D, 6 | I, 8 | J, 1 | F, 6 | B, 3 | I, 7 | F, 2 | J, 3 | H, 2 | I, 9 |
| G, 2 | B, 5 | I, 10 | E, 2 | J, 2 | G, 6 | B, 4 | E, 6 | B, 2 | J, 4 |

FIND THE BATTLESHIPS!

Your mission is to locate the enemy's five battleships. Using
the coordinates listed on the side, shade the lettered/
numbered grid to reveal where the ships are. Good luck!

CANDY LAND

Can you feel the refreshing minty breeze, and smell the chocolate? Welcome to Candy Land, where scrumptious treats are everywhere, and it's all about savoring each delicious moment!

Candy Castle

START

LOST IN GUMDROP MOUNTAINS!

Uh-oh! Mayor Mint has veered off the path while admiring the scenic views from Gumdrop Mountains. Can you help him find the correct path to the Candy Castle?

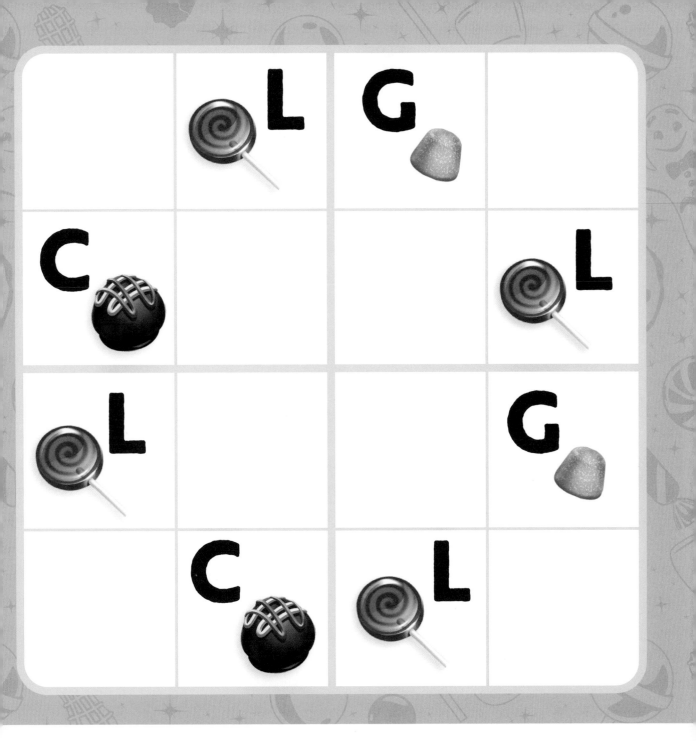

SWEET SUDOKU

Fill in the grid so that each column, row, and box has one
of each letter and draw in the correct sweet treat!

 C  L  I   G

CONNECT THE DOTS

King Kandy has a special surprise for Duchess E. Claire! Connect the dots to find out what it is. Can it be something sweet and delicious?

```
D A E R B R E G N I G E
P B C J O H E P C C C Q T
A O O A U G O S E E I A
F J P Y S R Q T J C T L
F R O I D T R O O R N O
M N O M L V L K L E I C
I Y U S T L B E L A M O
M G O Y T Z O F Y M R H
E W J C Y I A L P P E C
W P F K L A N C E E P A
L I C O R I C E A A P Y
S P R I N K L E S K E V
K I N G K A N D Y S P X
```

KING KANDY	LOLLIPOP	LICORICE	PEPPERMINT
ICE CREAM PEAKS	CHOCOLATE	FROSTINE	SPRINKLES
GINGERBREAD	GUMDROP	JOLLY	CASTLE

CANDY LAND WORD SEARCH

Look for the 12 sweet Candy Land words listed in the word bank.
You can find the words in all directions in the word search:
across, down, diagonally, and even backward!

RACE TO THE CASTLE!

King Kandy has just created a brand-new delicious treat: triple chocolate silk truffles with peppermint chocolate sprinkles! Mayor Mint, Princess Lolly, Jolly, and Duchess E. Claire each want to be the first to try it. Who will make it to the castle to taste this amazing confection?

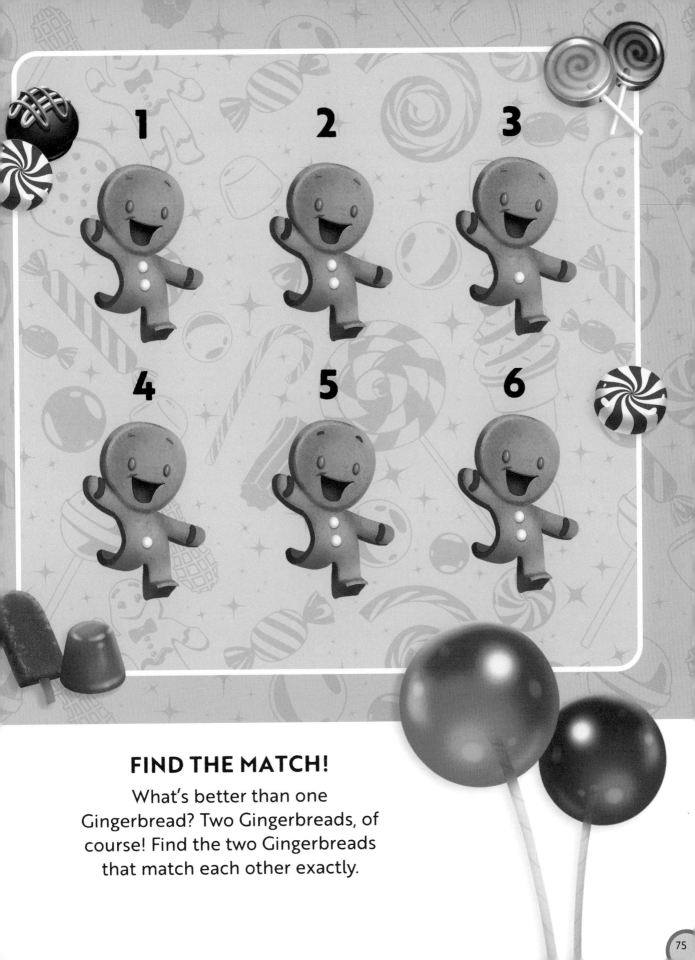

1

2

3

4

5

6

FIND THE MATCH!

What's better than one
Gingerbread? Two Gingerbreads, of
course! Find the two Gingerbreads
that match each other exactly.

ANSWER KEY

2
← START

3

```
Z V X X M X M S S   S H S
A R J E X M C S M O Y L I
R O N P I L O T L I D C D
E C T A M N F X P E N Z E
B V H I I O D E Y E E N S
R J M I N C M W E T T T I
A H U N T A I W R C A I G
B D U D R E J G R C K S N
G R I A G C C Q A K I T E
S W P I K E K T I M A T R
E R E T H G I F E R I F
N A I C I R T C E L E
A C C O U N T A N T C
V J H F B R E H C A E T
```

4
CANARY = ACTOR
DACHSHUND = CHEF
POODLE = FASHION DESIGNER
CHAMELEON = MUSICIAN
TARANTULA = SCIENTIST

6

7
Get ready to be amazing!

8

10
CAR

11

ACROSS	DOWN
2 CROWN	1 RING
3 PEARL	2 COPPER
5 EMERALD	4 GEMS
7 TIARA	6 DIAMOND
8 GOLD	10 SILVER
9 DAZZLING	
11 JEWEL	

12

13

14

15

S	H	D	C
C	D	S	H
H	S	C	D
D	C	H	S

16
ILLINOIS AVE = 58
WATER WORKS = 102
READING RAILROAD = 96
BOARDWALK = 26

17

18
The butler did it!

19

21

22

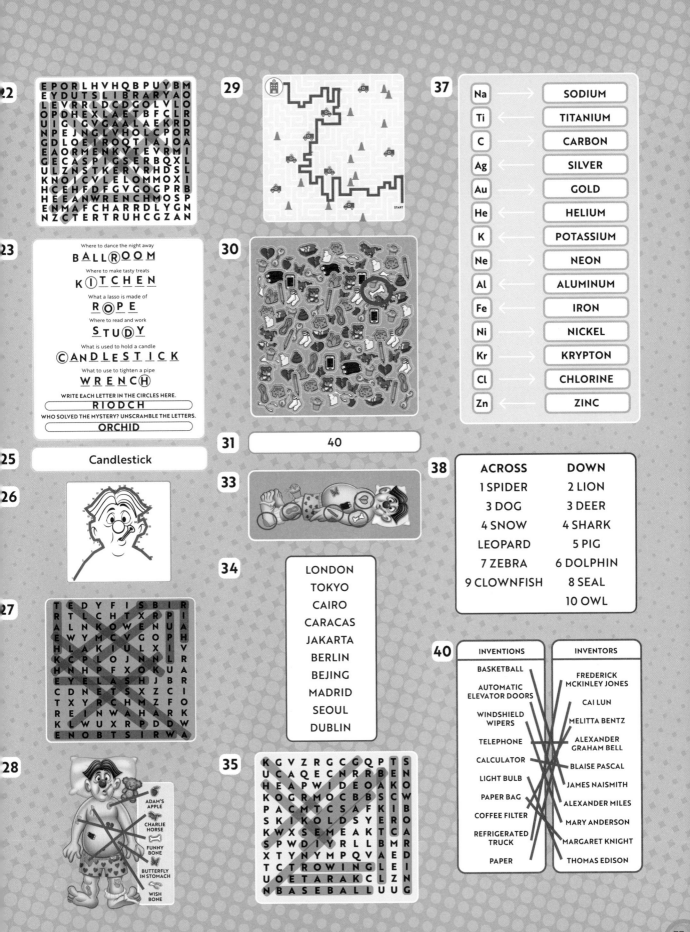

```
E P O R L H V H Q B P U Y B M
E Y D U T S L I B R A R Y A O
L E V R R L D C D G O L V L U
O P D H E X L A E T B F C L R
U I G I G V G A A L A E K R O
N P E J N G L V H O L C P O A
G D L O E I R O O T I A J O A
E A O R M E N K V T E V R M I
A C A S P I G S E R B Q X L L
U L Z N S T K E R V R H D S L
K N O I C V L E L O M M O X I
H C E H F D L V G O G P R R B
H E E A N W R E N C H M O S P
E N M A F C H A R R D L Y G N
N Z C T E R T R U H C G Z A N
```

23

Where to dance the night away
B A L L R(O)O M

Where to make tasty treats
K(I)T C H E N

What a lasso is made of
R(O)P E

Where to read and work
S T U(D)Y

What is used to hold a candle
(C)A N D L E S T I C K

What to use to tighten a pipe
W R E N C(H)

WRITE EACH LETTER IN THE CIRCLES HERE.
R I O D C H

WHO SOLVED THE MYSTERY? UNSCRAMBLE THE LETTERS.
O R C H I D

25

Candlestick

26

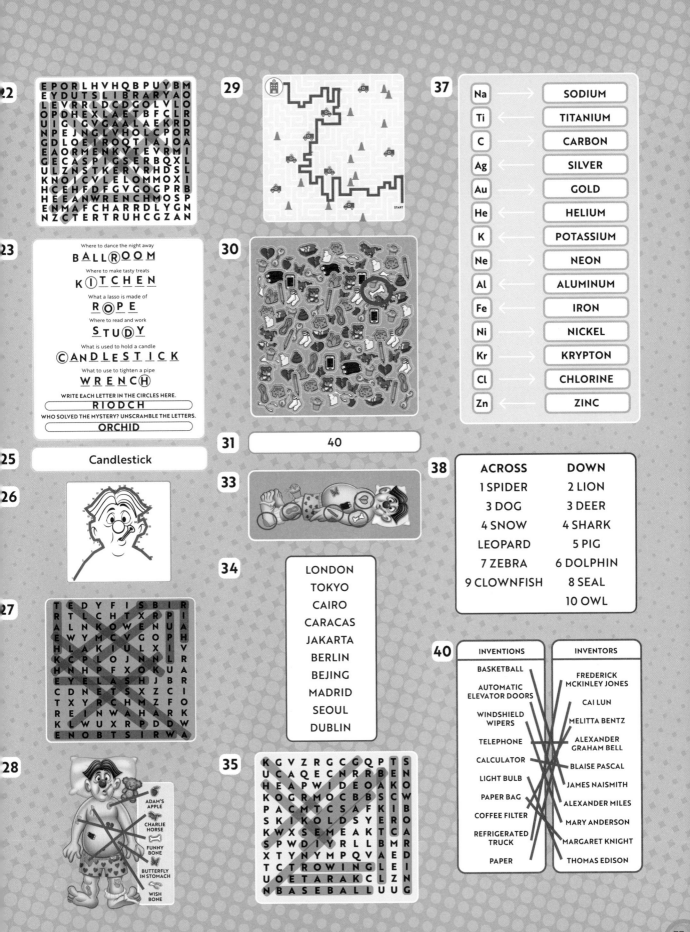

27

```
T E D Y F I S B I R
R T L C H T X R P I
A L N K O W E N U A
E W Y M C V G O P H
H K L A K I U L X V
H K C P L O J N N L
H N H P F X O K U A
E Y E L A S H J A R
C D N E T S X Z C R
T X Y R C H M Z F O
R E I N W A H A R K
K L W U X R P D M S
E N O B T S I R W A
```

28

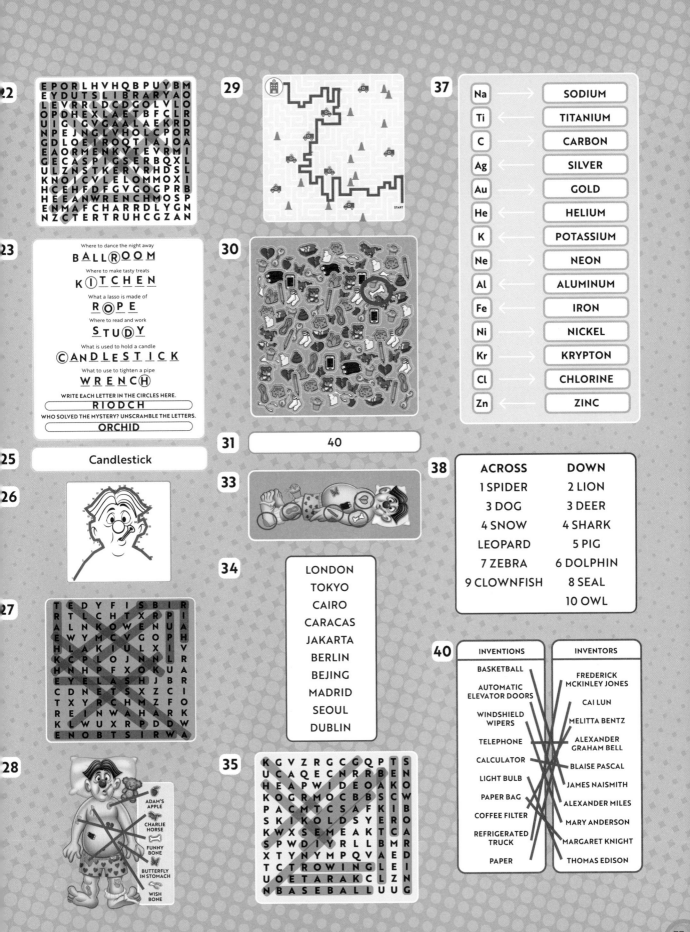

ADAM'S APPLE

CHARLIE HORSE

FUNNY BONE

BUTTERFLY IN STOMACH

WISH BONE

29

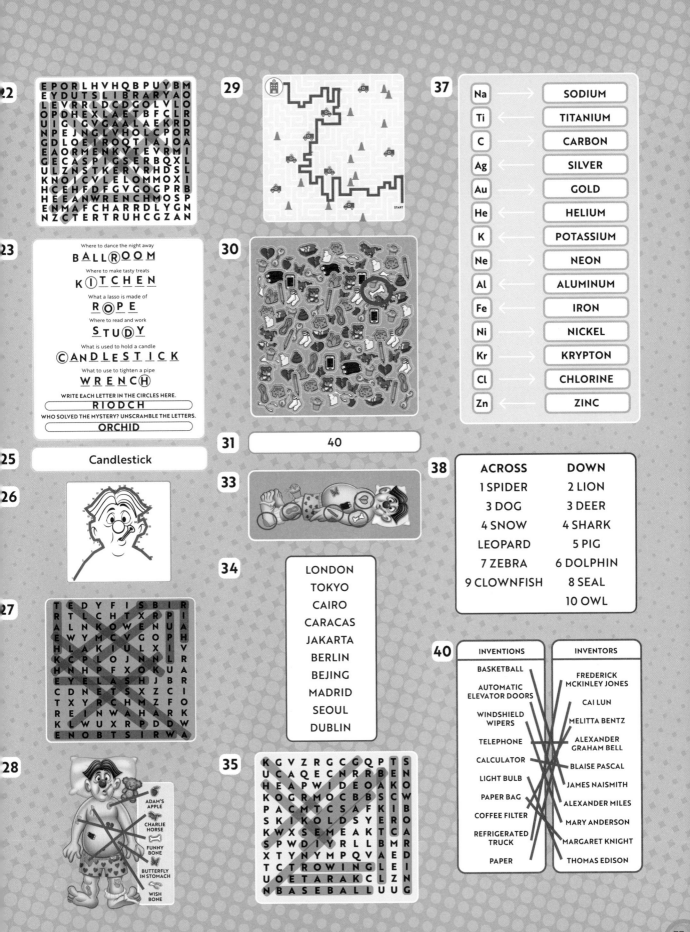

START

30

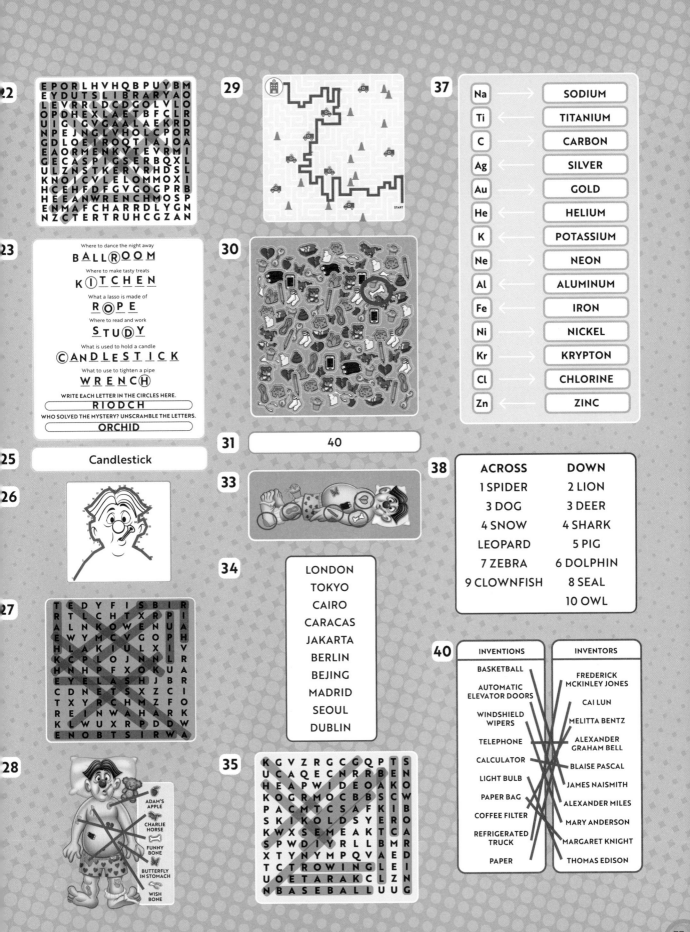

31

40

33

34

LONDON
TOKYO
CAIRO
CARACAS
JAKARTA
BERLIN
BEJING
MADRID
SEOUL
DUBLIN

35

```
K G V Z R G C G Q P T S
U C A Q E C N R R B E N
H E A P W I D E O A K O
K O G R M O C B B S C W
P A C M T C S A M I I B
S K I K O L D S Y E R O
K W X S E M E A K T C A
S P W D I Y R L L B M R
X T Y N Y M P Q V A E D
T C T R O W I N G L E N
U O E T A R A K C L Z N
N B A S E B A L L U U G
```

37

Na →	SODIUM
Ti ←	TITANIUM
C →	CARBON
Ag →	SILVER
Au →	GOLD
He ←	HELIUM
K →	POTASSIUM
Ne →	NEON
Al ←	ALUMINUM
Fe ←	IRON
Ni →	NICKEL
Kr →	KRYPTON
Cl →	CHLORINE
Zn ←	ZINC

38

ACROSS	DOWN
1 SPIDER	2 LION
3 DOG	3 DEER
4 SNOW LEOPARD	4 SHARK
7 ZEBRA	5 PIG
9 CLOWNFISH	6 DOLPHIN
	8 SEAL
	10 OWL

40

INVENTIONS	INVENTORS
BASKETBALL	FREDERICK MCKINLEY JONES
AUTOMATIC ELEVATOR DOORS	CAI LUN
WINDSHIELD WIPERS	MELITTA BENTZ
TELEPHONE	ALEXANDER GRAHAM BELL
CALCULATOR	BLAISE PASCAL
LIGHT BULB	JAMES NAISMITH
PAPER BAG	ALEXANDER MILES
COFFEE FILTER	MARY ANDERSON
REFRIGERATED TRUCK	MARGARET KNIGHT
PAPER	THOMAS EDISON

42

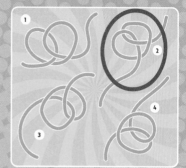

47

52

43

```
A Y F S U J H J X
T Z E J W A H G G R
D H D L N U K R E E
X E G D L A O K E E
R D E X Y R T F N N
N E X F R B E S T T
T N F R B X R I U U
B L U E T E X W T B
S T O O F L I T W R
A Q K A Z X W T B R
B X F S O K M V R F
```

48

Fresh fried fish, fish fresh fried, fried fish fresh, fish fried fresh

Poppy put a cup of proper coffee in a copper coffee cup

Crisp crusts crackle, crisp crusts crunch, crispy crackly crusts, crunch crunch crunch.

55

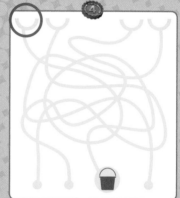

44

RF	RH	LH	LF
LF	LH	RF	RH
RH	RF	LF	LH
LH	LF	RH	RF

49

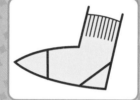

56

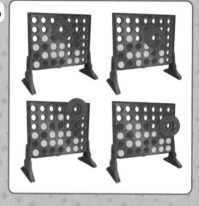

45

NO SOCKS!	CHANDELIER
GET A GRIP	BIGFOOT
FANCY LIGHTING	SECONDHAND
YETI	FOOTPRINTS
USED	BAREFOOT
TRACKS	HANDLE
DO AS YOU PLEASE	HANDSOME
GOOD LOOKING	MERCHANDISE
A FRIENDLY GESTURE	FOOTLOOSE
GOODS	SUREFOOTED
HAPPENING OR STARTING TO HAPPEN	HANDSHAKE
CONFIDENT	AFOOT

50

2	3	4	1
4	1	3	2
1	4	2	3
3	2	1	4

51

```
R A L P I L I T F
Z V J D A D T C E O
F C T A A Q T E N U
G O K N X L Q O C R
M I B L W R E U N J
P B M E U T G M O K
T E E N R O K M C W
J C N R F D B C Z
G O E O R U O F B E
C I U N S P O E E
E R X K N R T F I H
T E W G Q O U N W
Y C O N N E C T W
```

46

```
S K T S I R S D T U F E
T L H I A K E U H O O D
N X R D X R R V R Q H D
E R O E B N O W O D S N
C W U W Y L A U N G D I
A Y G A I R W I N G S M
J B H Y D C H P V D I T
D Z O S B E Y O N D N Q
A I V B E W M H R E F A
K X N V E R E D N U A U
Q F D O D M S S O R C A
C L O C K W I S E D M D
```

57

LEONARDO, RAPHAEL, DONATELLO, MICHELANGELO	THE BEATLES
JOHN, PAUL, GEORGE, AND RINGO	SUITS IN A CARD DECK
NORTH, SOUTH, EAST, WEST	SEASONS
SPRING, SUMMER, FALL, WINTER	COMPASS POINTS
WATER, EARTH, FIRE, AIR	TEENAGE MUTANT NINJA TURTLES
SPADES, CLUBS, HEARTS, DIAMONDS	FANTASTIC FOUR
HUMAN TORCH, INVISIBLE WOMAN, MR. FANTASTIC, THE THING	CLASSICAL ELEMENTS

Amy

64 Great job! You sank their battleship!

65
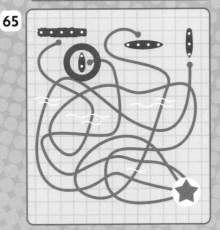

67

68

A	S	D	P
P	D	A	S
S	A	P	D
D	P	S	A

69

	1	2	3	4	5	6	7	8	9	10
A										
B										
C										
D										
E										
F										
G										
H										
I										
J										

71

I	L	G	C
C	G	I	L
L	I	C	G
G	C	L	I

72
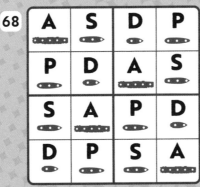

73

D A E R B R E G N I G E
P B C J O H E P C Q T A
A O O A U G O S E I O L
F J P Y S R Q T J R T O
F R O I D T R O O E N C
M N O M L V L K L C R O
I Y U S T L B E A I M H
M G O Y T Z O F Y M P C
E W J C Y I A L E E R A
W P F K L A N C E A E Y
L I C O R I C E A A S V
S P R I N K L E S K P X
K I N G K A N D Y S P X

74
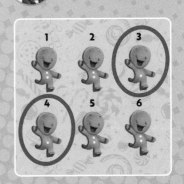
Jolly

75

BELGUIM
TANZANIA
CROATIA
NEPAL
ARGENTINA
LAOS
VANUATU
TURKEY
GREECE
GUATAMALA

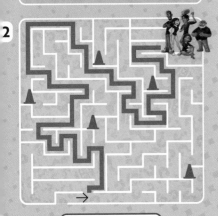

R W A R J V C E C L
L A O M I X E T O B
U C T O P A L U U L
K B L I Q P L L N U
H I S K U Q O F T E
N E M L G G G P R S
Q Y U Z Z A J C Y N
F S R U B O N A I P
P M D T R E C N O C
M I C R O P H O N E
A H A R M O N Y M G

INSIGHT
K I D S

PO Box 3088
San Rafael, CA 94912
www.insighteditions.com

Library of Congress Cataloging-in-Publication Data available.

ISBN: 978-1-64722-516-2

CEO: Raoul Goff
VP of Licensing and Partnerships: Vanessa Lopez
VP of Creative: Chrissy Kwasnik
VP of Manufacturing: Alix Nicholaeff
Executive Editor: Sara Miller
Executive Editor: Paul Ruditis
Art Director: Stuart Smith
Designer: Brooke McCullum
Editor: Elizabeth Ovieda
Managing Editor: Vicki Jaeger
Production Editor: Jan Neal
Senior Production Manager: Greg Steffen
Senior Production Manager, Subsidiary Rights: Lina s Palma

Additional art: P.39 Olga Potter/shutterstock.com

ROOTS of PEACE  REPLANTED PAPER

Insight Editions, in association with Roots of Peace, will plant two trees for each tree used in the manufacturing of this book. Roots of Peace is an internationally renowned humanitarian organization dedicated to eradicating land mines worldwide and converting war-torn lands into productive farms and wildlife habitats. Roots of Peace will plant two million fruit and nut trees in Afghanistan and provide farmers there with the skills and support necessary for sustainable land use.

Manufactured in China by Insight Editions

10 9 8 7 6 5 4 3 2 1